More Favorite
Songs of Praise

Solos, Duets, Trios with Optional Piano Accompaniment

Arranged by Michael Lawrence

CONTENTS

Alfred

© 2011 Alfred Music Publishing Co., Inc.
All Rights Reserved. Printed in USA.

ISBN-10: 0-7390-7709-0
ISBN-13: 978-0-7390-7709-2

Cover photo courtesy of Bill Davenport

AMAZING GRACE
(MY CHAINS ARE GONE)

Words and Music by
CHRIS TOMLIN and LOUIE GIGLIO
Arranged by MICHAEL LAWRENCE

FLUTE

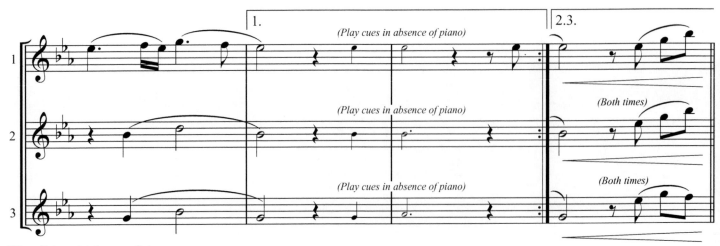

*Play all times in absence of piano.

37091

HE KNOWS MY NAME

Words and Music by
TOMMY WALKER
Arranged by MICHAEL LAWRENCE

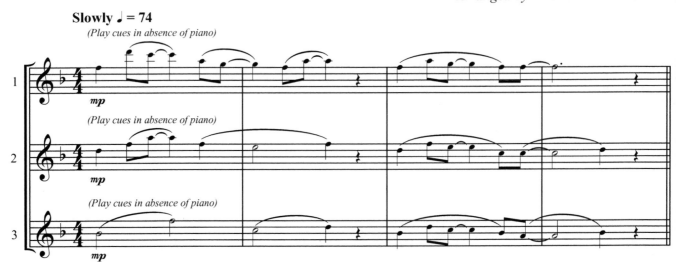

BETTER IS ONE DAY

Words and Music by
MATT REDMAN
Arranged by MICHAEL LAWRENCE

Rhythmically ♩ = 86

THE HEART OF WORSHIP
(WHEN THE MUSIC FADES)

Words and Music by
MATT REDMAN
Arranged by MICHAEL LAWRENCE

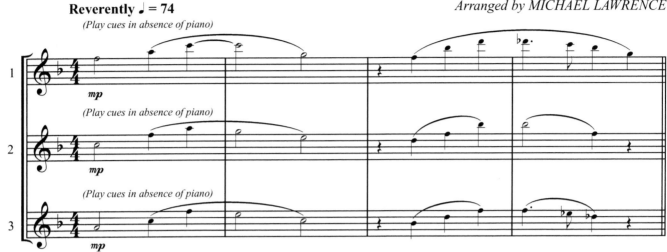

*Play both times in absence of piano.

HOLY IS THE LORD

Words and Music by
CHRIS TOMLIN and LOUIE GIGLIO
Arranged by MICHAEL LAWRENCE

*Play both times in absence of piano.

HOW GREAT THOU ART

Words and Music by
STUART K. HINE
Arranged by MICHAEL LAWRENCE

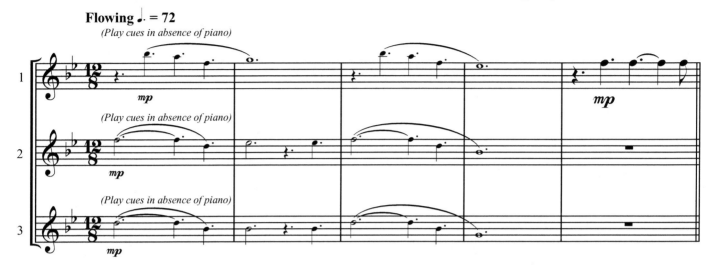

JESUS, NAME ABOVE ALL NAMES

Words and Music by
NAIDA HEARN
Arranged by MICHAEL LAWRENCE

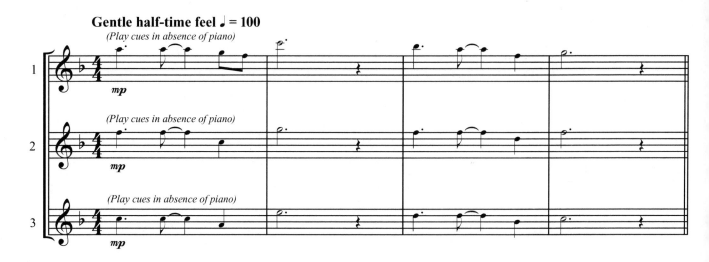

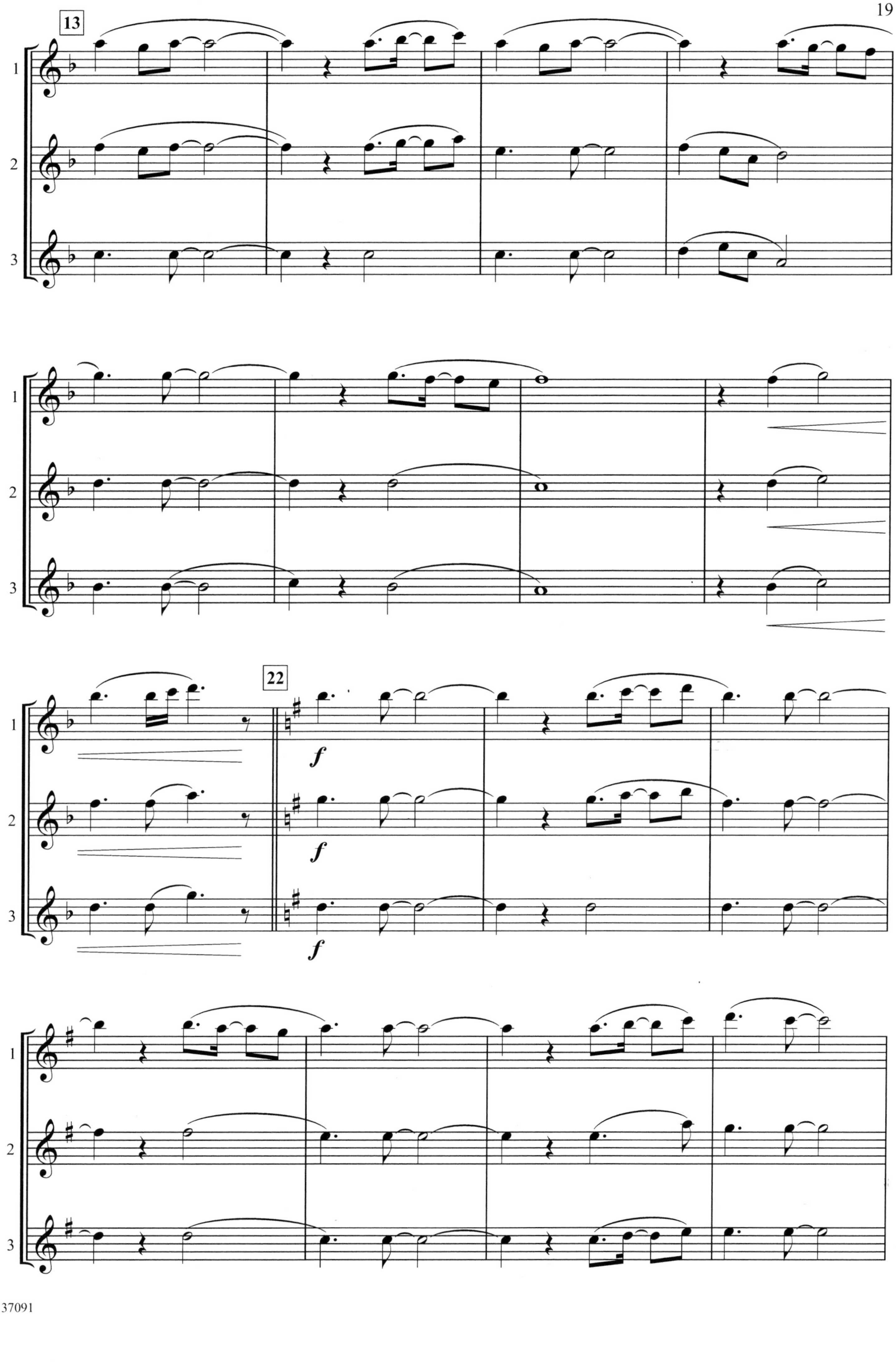
13
22
f

MADE ME GLAD

Words and Music by
MIRIAM WEBSTER
Arranged by MICHAEL LAWRENCE

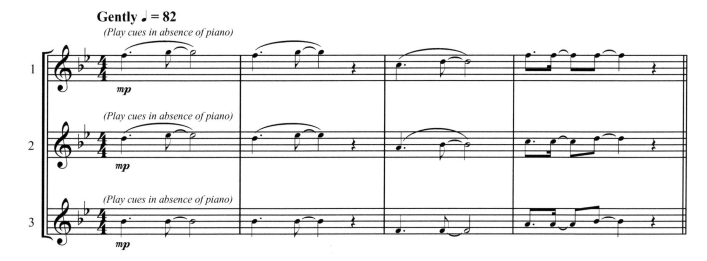

OPEN THE EYES OF MY HEART LORD

Words and Music by
PAUL BALOCHE
Arranged by MICHAEL LAWRENCE

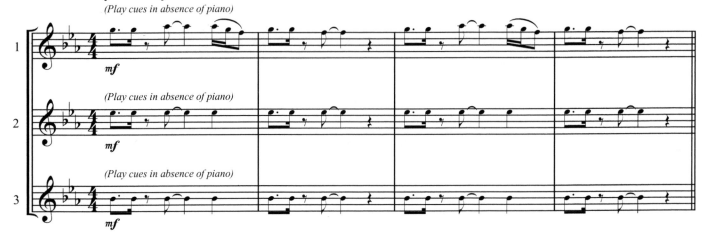

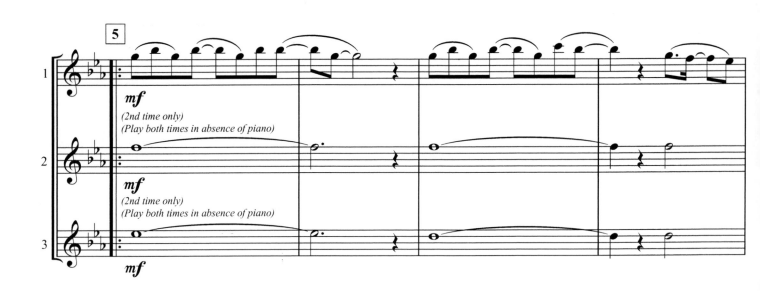

SING TO THE KING

Words and Music by
BILLY FOOTE
Arranged by MICHAEL LAWRENCE

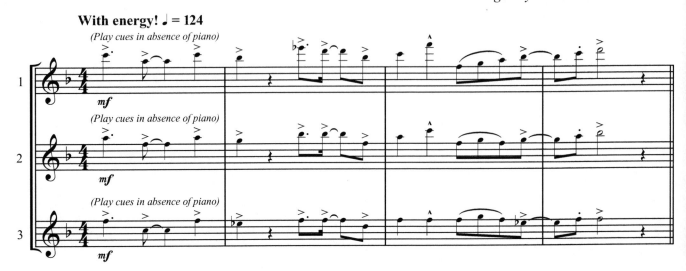

30

37091

YOU ARE MY ALL IN ALL

Words and Music by
DENNIS JERNIGAN
Arranged by MICHAEL LAWRENCE

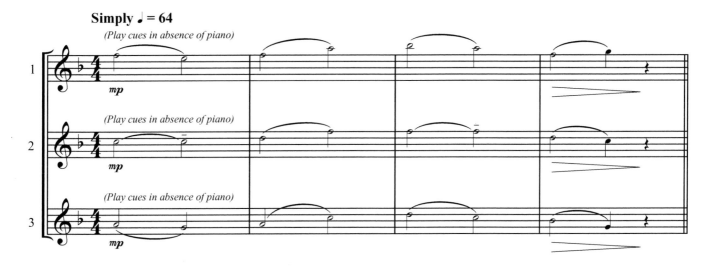

YOU'RE WORTHY OF MY PRAISE

Words and Music by
DAVID RUIS
Arranged by MICHAEL LAWRENCE

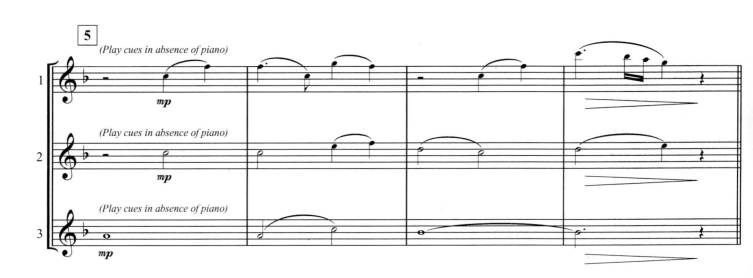